Darkness to

Darkness to

ODESIA BIRDEN

TATE PUBLISHING
AND **ENTERPRISES,** LLC

Published by Tate Publishing & Enterprises, LLC
127 E. Trade Center Terrace | Mustang, Oklahoma 73064 USA
1.888.361.9473 | www.tatepublishing.com

Tate Publishing is committed to excellence in the publishing industry. The company reflects the philosophy established by the founders, based on Psalm 68:11,
"The Lord gave the word and great was the company of those who published it."

Book design copyright © 2014 by Tate Publishing, LLC. All rights reserved.
Cover design by Rtor Maghuyop
Interior design by Caypeeline Casas

Published in the United States of America

ISBN: 978-1-63063-924-2
1. Religion / Christian Life / Spiritual Growth
2. Religion / Christian Life / Personal Growth
14.01.13

Dedication

❀

First and foremost, I would like to dedicate this book to God.

Secondly, to my mom and family.

Last but not least, to Sister Hollie and the people God has placed in my life, wicked and honorable. It's never too late to realize what's important in your life, but you must pray for it.

Chapter 1

❈

My name is Odesia. I was born on January 4, 1962, in the state of Louisiana. Before we read any further, let's pray the words Jesus taught His disciples, the Lord's Prayer:

> Our Father in heaven, hallowed be your Name. Your Kingdom come, your will be done on earth as it is in heaven. Give us today our daily bread,

and forgive us of our debts, as we also have forgiven our debtors. And lead us not into temptation, but deliver us from evil. For Yours is the kingdom and the power and the glory forever. Amen.

The following events are true and began in Ohio. These testimonies are intended for the believers to strengthen their faith. To the nonbelievers and the recovering addicts, the prize for all is heaven. I fully understand these days and times we all need to witness or read about a miracle that has happened in the twentieth century.

The fall of 1974, I was eleven years of age, one hundred pounds; had shoulder-length light-brown hair, medium complexion, dark eyes; and was four feet tall. The following depicts events regarding a predator, manipulation, drugs, and sex.

My first encounter with the enemy of our soul, Satan, I was raking leaves for money. It took hours to complete one yard, front and back. That day, I watched as a stranger in his window watched me. Once I completed raking that yard, I was paid. I began to walk away.

The stranger yelled, "Come over here!"

And my thoughts were, *Next house.*

The stranger's yard was full of leaves, so I went. He quoted a price of $20 to rake his yard. I thought to myself that was too high. In those days, $7–$10 was the normal amount for a front yard and backyard. I thought I had gotten lucky and wouldn't have to do another yard that day. Once I was finished with the stranger's yard, he paid me. Before I could walk away, he quoted another $20 to do his dishes.

The next day, I went there to work. The stranger's name was Michael. He was married and had a baby girl. His wife worked first shift, and he worked second shift. Michael was approximately 170 pounds, five feet eight, and had short dark hair and a dark complexion.

His daughter was sleeping while I washed dishes. While I was washing dishes, he kept asking questions—how old was I, what school did I attend, where did I live? I answered all his questions truthfully. He went on to say he had just celebrated his thirty-second birthday.

He then went to another part of the house, and soon I smelled marijuana. I knew the smell because two of my girlfriends, Lisa and Marilyn, smoked it. I never did. They would call me a square. Anyway, Michael came back to the kitchen. I was almost finished with the dishes. He had rolled up a joint of marijuana and insisted that I smoke with him, and then he would pay me. I felt intimidated and afraid of the tone that he used. Now all I wanted was to get out of his house. So again, he passed the joint to me, and I hit it a couple of times. He then insisted I finish the joint.

I smoked most of it and choked mostly. He then went to get my pay from another room of the house.

Seconds later, he returned, and I was sitting down. I couldn't keep my balance or keep my head up. I felt sick. It was then I could feel his breath on my neck, and I had no sense of control. I was too high to fight him off. With tears in my eyes, at once it was over. I was no longer a virgin.

I staggered home and told no one. I hated the rest of that year of 1974. Months later, it was January 1975, and four days later, it was my twelfth birthday. A week later, I started my period for the first time. Only my mother, Faye, my sister, Betty, my two friends Lisa and Marilyn knew because I only told the four of them.

It was early March 1975, and Lisa and Marilyn came over, and we went to Lisa's house. While we were in the backyard, Marilyn pulled out a half baggie of marijuana and pills.

Lisa said, "You are twelve, and that's when the both of us started smoking marijuana and doing pills." And if I wanted to continue being their friend, I would have to smoke as well.

"Your first time would be with us," they added.

I never told anyone I had smoked with Michael. The secret of what he did was eating me alive. So I smoked with Lisa and Marilyn. It was my second time ever being high, and I got sick and hungry, and they wouldn't walk me home. I only lived six blocks away, and I started walking slowly home before dark.

Michael was driving by. When he saw me, he backed up, got out of his car, and walked up to me. I froze. He started apologizing for what he did to me. I was full of downers and marijuana. Plus, I hadn't eaten. I felt light-headed.

Michael said, "You smell like marijuana, and you are high? I'll give you a lift home."

Without thinking, I got in his car. Too high to continue walking, I couldn't keep my focus or my head up, and when I finally looked up,

I saw we were pulling inside his garage. He pulled me out of his car and blocked the door. Once again, I was too high to fight him off. When it was over, I cried. He dropped me off a block from my house. Again, I told no one. If I had told, it would mean the abuse was real. I pretended it didn't happen and stayed high to numb the pain.

Months later, on December 20, 1975, I gave birth to a son. He was seven pounds, three ounces. Deshawn is his name. By the grace of God, he was healthy. Still I stayed high as often as I could. My mother and sister and friends thought my son belonged to one of the boys from the neighborhood. I never revealed a name, nor would I talk about it again.

We moved from that neighborhood when my son was four months old. By then, I was a junkie (using marijuana, uppers, and downers daily). I was faced with a situation I couldn't control, and being high was the only way I could deal with what happened. Michael became a thing of my past. He stole my dreams of becoming a part-time stewardess in order to pay my way through college.

I completed the sixth grade and dropped out during the seventh grade. I was too high to keep my grades up and wasn't focused at all. My son was six months old, and I had started a new school where one was allowed to bring their child. There were young mothers that were in somewhat of the same situation I was in.

Then it was time for my son's six-month checkup. I dressed my son first that morning. My mother was off from both jobs that day. That was unusual to be off from both jobs the same day. Anyway, I didn't think much of it. So I showered and got dressed for school. My mother stopped me. Her words were, "Go on to school, and I'll take the baby to the pediatrician." I smiled and went to school, not knowing that day would change my life.

When I got home from school, my mother was there alone, and she didn't say a word. I knew something was wrong but couldn't put my finger on it until many hours later. I never bothered asking my mother where my son was or what the pediatrician said because it was clear something was troubling her. I was doing my homework and hadn't been high for weeks. I thought to myself, *My son is with my sister.* My sister would care for her nephew as often as she could, taking him on long walks. She loves my son.

My sister arrived home alone.

My next thought, while doing homework, *My son is with my stepfather, Joe.* Joe would take my son on long drives, and usually when they would come back, my son would be asleep. Well, it was late in the evening, and my mother still hadn't said a word. When my stepfather arrived home, he was alone and drunk.

I went to my mother's bedroom and asked, "Where is my son?"

My mother's response was, "Sit down, we need to talk." Then she told me, "Your cousin came down from Michigan, and I packed all your son's belongings and sent him to Louisiana to stay with your aunt and uncle."

My whole world changed again. That day, I lost all respect for my mother. I never even got the chance to kiss my son and say good-bye to him.

My mother's reasoned, "You need to focus on school, and I can't afford day care, you, your sister, plus all the bills."

Her husband was a hustler, and it was not a guaranteed paycheck. My mother's dreams were to raise her two girls out of the state of Louisiana so we wouldn't have to grow up working in the fields, just as she had done. She wanted us to have the things other children had, and we did. My mother worked two jobs for as long as I can remember. Nothing was easy for her. All she accomplished, she worked for. That was one of my reasons I never revealed the name or age of my son's father. I didn't want to be the one to steal my mother's dreams for my sister and me.

My mother would wake us every morning on her way to work, except for weekends. My mother would return from her job in the evening, five days a week. This went on for decades. My mother wasn't really around to see us off to school, so she didn't have a clue whether we attended or not, at least until she received our report cards. And that's when she found out I had quit school during the seventh grade.

I started running away from home and continued to run away. I would call my mother so she would know I was alive and still upset because she sent my son away. From 1976 to 1979, it seemed like I had been incarcerated every year in juvenile. From 1982 to 2008 again, it seemed like I had been incarcerated every year in prison, although I felt I had served two life sentences.

Anyway, at thirteen, I met a stranger fresh out of the army. He was twenty-four years old, stood six feet, weighed 180 to 210 pounds, and had short hair and a dark complexion. His name was Hubert. I told him I was months away from my eighteenth birthday. One month later, I moved in with him.

During that time, I was incarcerated for weeks at a time because I was a runaway. I was living with him without anyone knowing my whereabouts. Hubert just thought I was going back and forth to home. He had no idea that I was in juvenile. He was used to me coming and going as I pleased. He was just an escape. It was never love. He had a one-bedroom apartment and worked a full-time job. He also sold marijuana and pills. He never got high. While he was at work, I sold the drugs. Hubert and I were sexually active almost every night.

It was my fourteenth birthday, and I can't remember when, but Hubert came home after work one day and told me my sister told him to tell me, if he had seen me, to tell me, "Happy fourteenth birthday." So I told him the truth concerning my age. He said I deceived him, and for days, he slept on the couch.

One morning before work, his words were, "We'll talk when I get home." I knew it was over. So I packed all my belongings without leaving a note. He would come by my mother's house, and I refused his visits mostly each and every time. And I started having morning sickness. I felt that way before when I was pregnant with my first son.

I told my mother. She made a doctor's appointment for me. The results were that I was once again pregnant at fourteen. I called Hubert and told him of the news, and still refused most of his visits. During my seventh month of pregnancy, Hubert saw me once. A few weeks later, my mother purchased a plane ticket to Louisiana.

It was January, my fifteenth birthday. Weeks later, my second son was born on January 27. He weighed six pounds, eight ounces. By God's grace, he too was healthy. I named him Demond.

The lifestyle I chose wouldn't allow me to care for my sons. Shortly after Demond's second birthday, I returned to Ohio, leaving both sons in Louisiana. I knew my aunts and uncles would give them the life I couldn't. I couldn't face reality because I wasn't used to living in it.

At fifteen, I felt ashamed until I heard a gospel radio station. The pastor was talking about conception. His words were, "Conception is of God, man is the donor," allowing me to let go of the shame. I came to believe my two sons were gifts from God.

That summer of 1977, I fell in love with my sons. My first thoughts were all I was to do was to protect them without love. I was confused, and it couldn't be done because I loved them both. By the way, I was too far gone. A junkie, and I knew nothing about motherhood or even about raising children. In order for my sons to have a chance at a good life, I signed them over to my aunts and uncles. Their chances of survival with me were slim. I forgave my mother. I became grateful and unashamed. I know now it was for their best interest. When it came to my sons, I saw their innocence. The ending to this testimony is over.

Three and a half decades later, Michael panhandles on the street and sleeps at a homeless shelter, dying of cirrhosis of the liver. Hubert is currently serving a life sentence for killing his wife. We all must pay for the decisions we make. I forgave them both. An eye for an eye leaves the whole world blind. All things truly wicked start from innocence.

Amen.

Chapter 2

❊

At age sixteen, months away from my seventeenth birthday, I ran away from Ohio to Louisiana trying to escape my many habits, only to learn there is no escaping Satan. I was one of his workers and recruited unsuspecting victims, just as Satan did me. Didn't matter to me the ages of the victims I recruited. Satan was my teacher, and I had grown to love him. When Satan showed up with a truckload of promises, it became hard to walk away. My journey began again. With deceit in my heart, I set out to find someone who had the means to support my many habits.

I met a stranger in his forties in a bar in Louisiana. His name was Perry. He was only in Louisiana to attend his grandfather's funeral. He was in town for three days. For three days, I was with him. He kept me high, and that's what I was after. The third day, he asked if I would like to live in Vegas.

"Why not?" I responded.

Across the state line I went. Two to three days after being in Vegas, I quickly found out he was a drug dealer, of powder cocaine, a drug I had heard about but never experienced. After a week of being in Vegas, Perry threw a party. Hours before the party, he took me to the salon and to the mall for some shopping. There were businessmen, models, and drug dealers. Ninety percent were junkies. Their baggies were filled with powder cocaine. Everyone mingled. Oh, by the way, Perry never took drugs.

Hours later, a young lady, probably in her midtwenties, came through the door. She was one of the prettiest women I had ever seen face-to-face. All eyes were on her. Her name was Ruby. She walked up to Perry and me and introduced herself. She was one of Perry's workers. At the end of the party, on her way out the door, she whispered to me, "Under the makeup, you are a child, but your secret is safe with me. Welcome to the big league." She added, "Perry takes care of no one for free."

A week after the party, she came by the house because Perry wanted to show me around Vegas and teach me what was expected of me. It was my seventeenth birthday. Perry came to my room. Although we were sexually active, we had different bedrooms. Ruby introduced me to powder cocaine.

In six months of using daily, I developed a dealer's habit and quickly stopped the use of marijuana and pills. I had found the drug of choice. Cocaine took me to a place Jesus wouldn't go.

Perry asked me to transport drugs to Reno, Las Vegas, and Los Angeles, California, which I did. It was the only way I could support my habit. Perry and I stopped all sexual activities, and I became one of his workers. Ruby's words were, "Remember, I told you, Perry takes care of no one for free."

I transported drugs for almost a year then my habit increased. It was my eighteenth birthday. That weekend, Perry gave me two bricks, meaning two keys of raw cocaine. I took one to Reno and broke down the second one. Taped it to my nude body and paid cash for a one-way plane ticket to Ohio. I wasn't safe until the plane was in the air. I knew I would never return to Vegas.

I left Vegas with the gym suit and gym shoes I had on, my purse, and a key of cocaine and money. I lined the outer baggies of cocaine with red pepper before the flight. Perry used me, and I used him. He knew nothing about Ohio. I was safe, and that became a memory. Once I arrived in Ohio, I quickly sold ounces of cocaine. I lived with my mother and sister who did not know of this behavior.

Months passed, almost a year, and I was out of money and drugs. Left with a dealer's habit, once again, I started looking for someone to support my expensive habit. I would only date drug dealers or blue-collar workers. This went on for decades. As my habit increased, so did my need for more money and drugs. So I began hustling, which cost five trips to prison. Each and every prison term, I witnessed somewhat of the same events I had read in the Bible in Romans 1:18–32. I have committed sins in my life, but there are two sins I would never commit by the grace of God. And those are murder and having sex with the same sex.

"A child lost, but not forever," said the Lord.

Eight years ago, in 2005, I met a man whom my mother introduced me to. His name is Pastor Jim DeJonghe. He spoke with a calm, soft voice. I saw peace in him. Even then in my darkness, he offered to pick me up for

Sunday service. I couldn't understand why. I was dressed and prepared for my first visit to Soul Winners for Jesus Christ Church. When I went, I heard Pastor Marc preach for the first time. I quickly began to relish the way he explained the words of God.

Once service was over, Pastor Jim dropped me off at home, and my mind kept drifting back to the Sunday message: "Satan owns the fence." It was amazing, and a couple of days later, Pastor Jim called to see if I wanted to attend Wednesday evening service.

"Yes," I responded.

For the first time, I heard the way Pastor Scott explained the words of God, the Bible. Again, I fell in love because I have never heard the words of God explained the way all three pastors explained the Bible. Each and every time, I was amazed, and I was learning about my Lord and Savior.

You will never leave Soul Winners the way you came. You leave each and every time with a little more knowledge of God's will and plans for your life. I now see the three pastors as the three wise men. They are true servants of God and teach His will and His plan of salvation.

Now with some knowledge of God, I will not die an uneducated junkie. I broke the cycle of back-and-forth incarceration. My last and final prison term was in 2008. Three years later was the last time I was high, on

October 10, 2011. That night, I took several sleeping pills and drank a half bottle of brandy. I locked my door with the chain in the latch, and I crawled into bed fully dressed. The clock read 9:45 p.m., and I prayed for forgiveness. My words to God were, "I can no longer deal with the life I felt I was dealt." My whole miserable life flashed in pieces in my mind. I cried until I drifted to sleep.

God sent me an angel during my sleep. Along with the desire to want a better life for myself, I strongly believe the Lord was saying to me I had to put one foot forward—and He doesn't care which one—in order to walk out the darkness. It is written in Hebrews 11:1:

"Now faith is confidence in what we hope for and assurance about what we do not see."

I woke up with those words in my mind. There comes a time in your life when a voice cries out in your mind and says, "Enough is enough." In the real world, Satan is not Prince Charming, and you arc not Cinderella. With Satan, there aren't any happy endings. Happily ever after begins and ends with God. The dream Michael took from me three and a half decades ago, Jesus gave anew, a dream that no human can take away.

We just have to surrender our all to God, and He will show us His plan for us, which is

His best for our lives. He says so in Jeremiah 29:11–13:

> "For I know the plans I have for you", declares the LORD, "plans to prosper you and not to harm you, plans to give you hope and a future. Then you will call on me and come and pray to me, and I will listen to you. You will seek me and find me when you seek me with all your heart."

I now know that I will be happy in this life and supremely happy with the Lord forever in the next life. I fully understand that God sent His very best work, His Son, and we will never experience a greater love as long as we live. This life will be over soon. Heaven lasts always, amen!

By the way, no person can count all eternity. Eternity is forever, which also means heaven is forever.

On October 11, 2011, I said my final goodbyes to Satan and repented. It was clear I had to turn from the evil and be fully reconciled with my Lord and Savior, Jesus Christ, and therefore know that I will spend eternity in heaven with my Heavenly Father, not spend all eternity in hell. Praise God for that promise. You see, God wants all mankind to be reconciled back to Him, which is why He gave the only atonement for sin, His Son, Jesus. The Bible says in Romans 3:23, "For all have sinned and fall short of the glory of God." All are born in sin because of Adam and Eve. The good news is there is a way out, which is Jesus Christ, who bore our sins, shame, and healing. Everything we need was done by Jesus's crucifixion at the cross on Calvary.

Somehow I felt I was living someone else's life. Jesus showed me the gates of hell, and I saw where I was headed. Not so anymore! I will forever walk on the streets of gold in heaven with my Lord and Savior, Jesus Christ. The Bible says, in Romans 8:37, we are more than conquerors: "Yet in all these things we are more than conquerors through him who loved us."

Jesus gave me a new lease on life on earth so that I can spend eternity with Him and also share with others what He has done for me and for them. The Bible says in John 14:6 that Jesus is the way and the truth and the life. No one comes to the Father except through Jesus. Think about this: we can't get in to see the movie at the movie theater if we don't first purchase the movie ticket. Jesus is our answer to be able to get into heaven at the end of our life here on earth.

On November 4, 2011, it was my fourth time in rehabilitation at the Nova House. This time I paid close attention and learned to chase recovery as I previously chased the drugs. It takes true strength to ask for help.

On December 2, 2011, I was released from the Nova House, and three days later, I started school, studying for my general equivalency diploma (GED). I will remain in school until I obtain my certificate.

I'd like to share this thought: I planted a garden. Each and every time I died, I went to God in need of a solution in order to help my garden grow. In a dream, I believe it was the Holy Spirit. That morning, I woke up and weeded out all the weeds, even though I tried to keep some old friends that weren't any good for my garden. This is why the garden would die. I started with fresh soil, new and positive people. Now my garden is healthy, beautiful, and strong. You can't hold on to the past.

I'm Odesia, and that garden is me.

On December 2011, I began cleaning out God's temple, which is me. This is what 1 Corinthians 3:16 says: "Don't you know that you yourselves are God's temple and that God's Spirit dwells in your midst?" I stopped all sexual activity, along with other things. If I could merit my own salvation, Christ would never have died to prove it. He rose in three days, a body that could not remain in the tomb. No amount of self-improvement or good deeds can win back what Adam lost.

I left my sons for a life unknown, and I never knew my Heavenly Father would have carried my load. I would like to one day stand face-to-face with John Wesley McGhee, Aretha Dee McGhee, Carrie Mae Smith, and Thomas C. Smith and thank them and let them know how much I love them. The first three are deceased. They raised both my sons from infants to adults without any support from me. For that, I am eternally grateful. Thank you!

There was a time in my life I'd only attend a church where the pastor had to be a black man. I now know and believe through the three pastors, the Holy Spirit speaks. The teachings will lead us to Jesus and the belief of a life spent in Heaven. I finally know what real love feels like. I knew if I continued going back to Soul Winners for Jesus Christ Church, I would hear the Holy Spirit speak.

The three pastors are Caucasian, a race I hated without reason only because of the color of their skin, along with my ignorance. A light came on in my head, and I came to the knowledge that all our DNA is different; however, we share the same bloodline as Christ. This makes us sisters and brothers in Christ, children of God. Of course, this is only possible once we confess our sins and ask Jesus to live in us, in our hearts, and believe that He rose on the third day and is alive. It's not their race, it's their faith. Praise God!

The pastors and members have patiently shared in my struggles. They understood my silent cries. Never did they turn their backs on me. They kept believing and praying that if I'd allow God to be the leader of my life, I would change my lifestyle. God doesn't make that decision for us. He allows us to make that decision.

On June 27, 2012, I was baptized, which is an outwardly acknowledgment, a sign telling the world that I am in Christ. He is mine, and I am His. Jesus was baptized openly; therefore, we are to be baptized openly and show the world.

That was the first day of the rest of my life. Hours before the baptism, I was reminded by a servant of God, Sister Edina, that Satan owns the fence. That day was the first time I

saw the beauty in her life. She is always will-
ing to pass it on. The knowledge she has in
the Bible is all in the name of love. When she
said that, I smiled, believing God's servants
were all around me.

Once inside the church, I got dressed for
my baptism. As I walked on to the altar into
the water, there stood Pastor Scott. All the
questions he asked, all I could say was yes.
When I fell back into the water, my body
totally relaxed. I trusted that Pastor Scott
would catch me if I should fall deeper. It was
so amazing. He held on to me as if it was the
Lord Almighty who had baptized me. He is
a servant of God.

While under the water, I could hear the people singing to heaven words of praise while witnessing my baptism. Once I came up from the water, there stood another servant of God to hug and greet me to my new life, Sister Suchi. After it was all over, I was dropped off at home.

In the wee hours in the morning, June 28, during my sleep, I heard my name. It wasn't the Holy Spirit, it was God. I knew because He called me by name. Please read and study 1 Samuel 3:4–10.

"Heavenly Father," I said, and He called me His miracle child. I smiled.

God said, "You will stand face to face with my Son."

I replied by saying, "Thank you, now I can rest."

It was a dream that one day will come true. Amen.

My two biggest supporters through it all has first been God, and I am honored to call Him Father. My second biggest supporter is my mother, Faye, whom I am proud to call Mom. The last eight years, my supporters have also been my pastors, the church members, and I am proud to call them all family. Amen.

I now see the beauty in the sinful world that God has created. I see through the eyes of my Lord, Jesus Christ. We all must protect our children from the wickedness of the world so they can reach their potential in Christ and be the children our Heavenly Father has ordained them to be before the foundations of world. As Psalm 139:16 says, "All the days ordained for me were written in your book before one of them came to be."

The following I dedicate to my sister, Betty. I never knew all those days of jump rope, jacks, and backyard play games. How I loved her funny special ways. Also for all those nights we fell asleep on the promises we'd never keep and secrets dark and deep. Through it all, you have been my first friend with a love that seems to have no end. My dearest gift from God was when He made us sisters. A poem by Judith Bond. Amen.

I now understand it. You learn the importance of loving yourself. A sense of newfound confidence is born. A sense of serenity is born from acceptance. You stop judging and pointing fingers. You begin to accept people as they are and overlook their shortcomings. Through all this a sense of peace and contentment is also born out of forgiveness. Amen.

For me, every day (365 days a year) I must give Him praise. God and my desire are the reasons I am no longer an addict. He gives us unending love and amazing grace. Now that I stand in the presence of Christ, I wonder how He could love me, a sinner. Jesus said in John 8:32, "Then you will know the truth, and the truth will set you free."

Allow me to leave you with this message. Jesus carried a cross I now wear. I'm not the trendsetter of the wooden cross. Jesus carried it first. To God be the glory to the happy ending of my story. Amen.